Bettendorf Public
Information Center
www.bettendorflibrary.com

S0-BAJ-318

WITHDRAWN

21ST-CENTURY ECONOMICS

UNDERSTANDING GLOBALIZATION

CHET'LA SEBREE

Cavendish
Square
New York

Published in 2020 by Cavendish Square Publishing, LLC
243 5th Avenue, Suite 136, New York, NY 10016

Copyright © 2020 by Cavendish Square Publishing, LLC

First Edition

No part of this publication may be reproduced, stored in a retrieval system,
or transmitted in any form or by any means—electronic, mechanical,
photocopying, recording, or otherwise—without the prior permission
of the copyright owner. Request for permission should be addressed to
Permissions, Cavendish Square Publishing, 243 5th Avenue, Suite 136,
New York, NY 10016. Tel (877) 980-4450; fax (877) 980-4454.

Website: cavendishsq.com

This publication represents the opinions and views of the author based on
his or her personal experience, knowledge, and research. The information
in this book serves as a general guide only. The author and publisher
have used their best efforts in preparing this book and disclaim liability
rising directly or indirectly from the use and application of this book.

All websites were available and accurate when this book was sent to press.

Library of Congress Cataloging-in-Publication Data

Names: Sebree, Chet'la, author.
Title: Understanding globalization / Chet'la Sebree.
Description: First edition. | New York : Cavendish Square, 2020. |
Series: 21st-century economics | Includes bibliographical references and index.
Identifiers: LCCN 2018048287 (print) | LCCN 2018050841 (ebook) |
ISBN 9781502645982 (ebook) | ISBN 9781502645975 (library bound) |
ISBN 9781502645968 (pbk.)
Subjects: LCSH: Globalization--Economic aspects--Juvenile literature.
Classification: LCC HF1365 (ebook) | LCC HF1365 .S43 2020 (print) |
DDC 337--dc23
LC record available at https://lccn.loc.gov/2018048287

Editorial Director: David McNamara
Copy Editor: Nathan Heidelberger
Associate Art Director: Alan Sliwinski
Designer: Joe Parenteau
Production Coordinator: Karol Szymczuk
Photo Research: J8 Media

Portions of this book originally appeared in
How Globalization Works by Laura La Bella

The photographs in this book are used by permission and through the courtesy
of: Cover metamorworks/Shutterstock.com; p. 4 wavebreakmedia/Shutterstock.
com; p. 6 Khun Ta/Shutterstock.com; p. 8 Uladzik Kryhin/Shutterstock.com;
p. 10 Kiro Popov/Shutterstock.com; p. 12 Kaidor/Wikimedia Commons/
File:Silk Road in the I century AD - en.svg/CC BY-SA 4.0; p. 15 Philippe Lissac/
Godong/Corbis Documentary/Getty Images; p. 17 Bascar/Shutterstock.
com; p. 19 NATALIA KOLESNIKOVA/AFP/Getty Images; p. 20 Martin Good/
Shutterstock.com; p. 22 Lester Balajadia/Shutterstock.com; p. 25 mariakraynova/
Shutterstock.com; p. 27 TONY KARUMBA/AFP/Getty Images; p. 29 moj0j0/
Shutterstock.com; p. 32 mark stephens photography/Shutterstock.com; p. 34
Malgosia S/Shutterstock.com; p. 39 Dominik Bindl/Getty Images; p. 41 MPI/
Archive Photos/Getty Images; p. 45 anouchka/E+/Getty Images; p. 48 Rawpixel.
com/Shutterstock.com; p. 51 ©iStockphoto.com/solidcolours; p. 53 MN Chan/
Getty Images; p. 54 Frans Delian/Shutterstock.com; p. 58 Bloomberg/Getty
Images; p. 62 Alexandros Michailidis/Shutterstock.com; p. 66 Janossy Gergely/
Shutterstock.com; design elements throughout Champ008/Shutterstock.com.

Printed in the United States of America

CONTENTS

THE WORLDWIDE EFFECT

Have you ever stopped to think about where the goods you purchase come from? When you look at the tags in your clothes, do some of them say "Made in El Salvador"? What about your favorite childhood toys? Have you ever wondered why so many are made in China? Have you ever considered why your town's grocery store makes it clear when produce is "locally sourced"? Maybe it's because those avocados are from the Dominican Republic, Peru, Colombia, or Indonesia. These are signs of globalization.

Opposite: Sometimes the vegetables at local markets are from nearby farmers. Other times, they may come from farmers from around the world.

The McDonald's Effect

"Globalization" is a term that became popular in the 1980s. It describes the increased international influence or movement of people, knowledge, ideas, products, and money. All of this movement has increased the interconnectedness among the world's populations. It has also made the merging of economic, political, social, and cultural identities possible.

Take a look at McDonald's, the largest fast-food chain in the world. It is an example of how a company might approach globalization. McDonald's operates more

In Saudi Arabia, McDonald's restaurants have different lines for men and women because public spaces are segregated, or separated, by gender.

than thirty-six thousand restaurants in over one hundred countries. Each day, it serves millions of people worldwide. But what is unique about McDonald's is that, throughout the world, its menus reflect the cultures of the countries in which it has restaurants.

In the United States, the most popular menu items are the Big Mac, Chicken McNuggets, and the chain's famous french fries. In India, however, many people do not eat beef due to their religious beliefs, which include honoring cows as sacred animals. For that reason, you won't find hamburgers on the menu at a McDonald's there. Instead, the menu features fish, chicken, and the most popular item, the veggie burger. This hamburger-like sandwich is made from potatoes, peas, and carrots, and is flavored with Indian spices.

The same consideration for local tastes and customs is extended to McDonald's branches around the world. The restaurant is an example of an American company growing beyond its borders while making sure that local customs are reflected in its menus. This, too, is globalization.

How It Works

Globalization occurs when companies, products, and services based in one country spread to other countries. This starts influencing the cultures and people in those

While Apple has a facility in California that designs new technology (pictured here), the company also has factories that produce and manufacture their products in China.

countries. The process of globalization can begin when there is a demand for a product that a particular country doesn't have or cannot produce. It can also begin when a company sets up factories in a different country.

Globalization is not a new concept. In the American colonies, the East India Company, which was established in Great Britain, brought cotton, silk, dye, and tea to America's shores for sale. Similarly, Russia was a major supplier of fur pelts to western Europe and parts of Asia. However, the pace, scope, and scale of globalization accelerated dramatically during the twentieth century in part because of advances in technology. In the twenty-first century, there are countless examples of products that are produced in other countries and sold globally. Sometimes, the company that designs the product is based in a different country from that in which the product is actually made. That product may be sold in a third country or even worldwide. For instance, the ever-popular iPhone is largely made and assembled in China, even though Apple is an American company based in California.

The Impact

Globalization has both positive and negative effects. It can create business opportunities for growing companies, which can result in new jobs. It gives people access to products and services that they might not otherwise have in their own countries. Additionally, it can aid in a new understanding of cultures, languages, and customs that are different from our own.

But globalization has downsides, too. It can cause a loss of native cultures and heritage as people adapt to foreign influences. It can cause job losses in some countries as businesses move their operations to other countries where it costs less to pay workers. This has a complex effect because it can help some countries grow and expand their workforce while costing another country much-needed jobs. Globalization can also harm the environment. Overall, globalization is a powerful economic force.

CHAPTER 1

DEFINING GLOBALIZATION

Globalization has taken off in our high-tech world. In the early nineteenth century, people communicated with each other by sending a letter or a telegram. By 1876, Alexander Graham Bell, creator of the telephone, placed his first phone call. By the end of the next century, we had developed new ways to reach out to each other instantaneously, even to people in countries on the other side of the world. Today, cell phones, email, text messaging, webcams, and the internet allow us to share our ideas immediately with others. In moments, a person sitting in her home in Wilmington, Delaware, can reach a friend in Bangkok, Thailand, via applications like Skype or WhatsApp. Similarly, a person can order something

Opposite: The movement of money across borders also affects the movement of people. As jobs and industries leave countries, people are left without work or means for survival.

from a different country through Amazon or Etsy and receive it in a matter of days. Although globalization is booming in the twenty-first century, these concepts aren't necessarily new.

Types of Globalization

Globalization stretches far back to the first trade relationships between countries. For instance, the Silk Road was an ancient trade route that extended between China and the Roman Empire. It led to the transfer of goods, in addition to the transmission, or spread, of

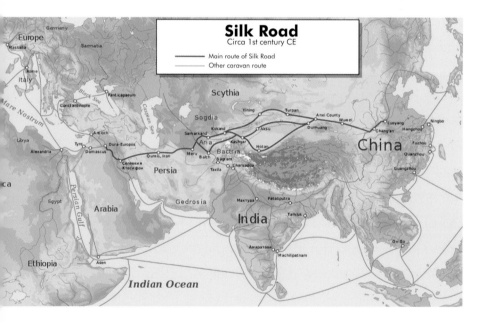

In addition to the spread of goods, many historians believe the Silk Road was responsible for the spread of the Black Death, a plague that devastated Europe in the mid-1300s.

new religions like Christianity and Buddhism. These are examples of economic and cultural globalization.

There are three main types of globalization: economic, political, and cultural. All of these forms of globalization, however, have to do with the transmission of things— whether they be physical things or beliefs—across international borders. Examining and understanding each of them allows us to see how globalization works in many ways. It also lets us see how nations and their cultures affect one another.

Type 1: Economic Globalization

When we use the words "economic globalization," we are really talking about how money travels around the world. Each country has its own businesses, and these businesses often sell their products outside of their own country. When people from many countries around the world are able to buy products that are made and sold by foreign companies—and even work for these companies in some cases—a connection is forged among many different nations and their cultures.

Economic globalization has been occurring for several thousand years, but it occurs more and with greater ease in our increasingly high-tech world. For many companies that make large products, production might occur in more than one country. Cars are often produced in multiple countries by different teams of workers. A new car may be designed in one country, its parts could be manufactured in a second country, and the assembly of those parts might occur in a third. The breakdown or separating out of jobs, which often increases efficiency, is called division of labor.

For example, Toyota Motor Company is a Japanese carmaker that has manufacturing and assembly factories in more than twenty-five countries, including the United States, Mexico, France, Brazil, Turkey, and Thailand. This division of labor in multiple countries affects globalization in two ways. The presence of these factories worldwide spreads a company's influence. Additionally, workers who receive paychecks in these nations now have the money to spend on products made both inside and outside of their home countries.

Another form of economic globalization occurs when companies in one country produce more goods and services than can be used by its own population. The Ivory Coast, located in Africa, is one of the largest producers of cocoa. It sells what it cannot use to other countries that need it. Countries will often pay for goods and services that either they cannot make themselves or are of a higher quality than what they can manufacture.

Other times, countries cannot produce enough of a product that is in great need, so they buy products from other countries. This is the case with the United States and its need for oil. The country produces a sizeable amount of oil. For instance, in September 2016 the United States was the world's top oil producer. However, the United States exports some of its oil, which means it sells some of its product abroad. Additionally, the United States still needs more than it produces, so it must import, or purchase, oil from other countries to fill demand.

Economic globalization is one of the few types of globalization that can be clearly measured. We can look

The Ivory Coast's main export is cocoa, drying in this image above.

at four different categories to see if economic globalization has increased or decreased. These four categories are:

- goods and services, which are measured in terms of the number of products that are exported or imported;
- migration, or movement of people, which allows us to watch how many people come into a country to find work or how many are forced to leave to find work outside that country;
- capital, or money, which helps gauge how much each nation makes as a result of products and people flowing back and forth;
- technology, which tells us how inventions and innovations in communication, computers, and manufacturing influence globalization.

Type 2: Political Globalization

Political globalization is another type of globalization, which focuses on the interactions between countries. Essentially, it is how governments from different countries get along with one another. For instance, the United States has countries that it is very friendly with (such as England, France, Japan, and Canada) and other countries that it is not so friendly with (like Iran and North Korea).

A good example of political globalization is the United Nations. Established in 1945, the organization

In 2018, the United Nations was made up of 193 member states.

was developed to support the international community. The organization's charter, or founding document, is fairly general so that "the United Nations can take action on the issues confronting humanity … such as peace and security, climate change, sustainable development, human rights, disarmament, terrorism, humanitarian and health emergencies, gender equality, governance, food production, and more," according to its website. In other words, the organization has a broad reach.

This is a good example of political globalization because the United Nations is made up of nearly two hundred countries. Each country has its own separate politics and government. However, these countries work together to promote a strong international community. The relationships formed by political organizations like this one can be helpful when we form partnerships to help defend ourselves against common enemies. They can also offer help following a natural disaster such as a hurricane or earthquake. Additionally, these sorts of political ties can lead to the exchange of scientific information like cures for diseases.

Type 3: Cultural Globalization

Cultural globalization refers to the sharing of ideas and cultural products. The United States is the largest exporter of movies and, thus, is a large exporter of American culture. Other countries produce films too. In fact, India produces more films a year than Hollywood does. Japan and Hong Kong are leaders in movie production as well. However, many of these films are not seen outside of their home countries. Indian films are produced mostly for Indian audiences. Films from Japan and Hong Kong are shown outside of Asia in art-house theaters that specialize in more artistic or experimental films. Foreign films often have trouble getting distributed and shown in the United States. However, streaming services like Netflix have made this easier.

Hollywood movies may showcase American ways of life, but even the United States' film industry is not entirely American. Hollywood is known for finding the best actors, actresses, and directors from around the world and making them stars. *Riverdale* star KJ Apa is from New Zealand, *Star Wars'* Daisy Ridley is from England, and *Black Panther's* Lupita Nyong'o is Mexican and Kenyan. Similarly, some of Hollywood's biggest studios are also foreign-owned. For example, Japan's Sony Company owns Columbia Pictures.

As cultural ideas are shared around the world, more people adopt them. As more people adopt them, the more normalized these cultural elements become. Think about types of cuisine, styles of clothing, and genres of music made popular throughout the world.

Cultural globalization can lead to economic globalization. Here, a group of actors celebrate the premiere of the American film *Transformers: Dark of the Moon* in Russia.

THE REGULATION OF GLOBALIZATION

Although there is no formal body that regulates globalization in its many forms, international organizations and individual countries contribute to the regulation of economic, political, and cultural globalization.

For instance, the World Trade Organization (WTO) is the singular global organization regulating international trade relationships, which affect economic globalization. The organization's goal is to manage these relationships

The World Trade Organization is based in Geneva, Switzerland.

through overseeing trade negotiations. It also implements and monitors trade policies, while settling international trade disputes. Additionally, the WTO is committed to helping developing countries to increase trade opportunities. Over 150 nations, representing 98 percent of the world's trade, are members of the WTO.

Similarly, the United Nations works to ensure a friendly global community. For example, the Paris Agreement is a pact signed by many United Nations members to combat the effects of climate change. The international agreement is an example of political globalization.

Individually, countries also have the capacity to control cultural and economic globalization. For instance, a country can place a tariff, or tax, on a foreign good to make it more expensive to import. In fact, a country can ban the importation of certain goods if it decides those goods are harmful to its citizens or have a negative effect on its economy. Similarly, a country can block websites. For instance, many sites such as Google, Facebook, Instagram, and WhatsApp are banned by the Chinese Central Cyberspace Affairs Commission. This government organization regulates and censors the internet in China, limiting the effects of cultural globalization.

McDonald's

BILLIONS AND BILLIONS SERVED

Drive-Thru

$1 ICE CREAM
CONES

CHAPTER 2

CAUSES AND EFFECTS

Sometimes the reach of globalization is hard to wrap our minds around. Here are some examples that might help. McDonald's serves more than sixty-five million people every day throughout the world. That's more than double the number of people who lived in Australia in 2016. Amazon employs more people internationally than the number of people who occupy small countries like the Bahamas and Belize. Every year, Domino's Pizza earns enough money in international sales to support the economies of several nations, including Bolivia and Iceland. Even with those concrete examples, globalization's reach can still feel mind-boggling.

Opposite: In 1994, McDonald's announced that it would stop counting how many burgers were sold as the company had sold over ninety-nine billion worldwide.

What Causes Globalization?

Globalization occurs for many reasons. In ancient times, it was a way to move resources that peoples in different areas had or needed. In the modern world, it works in much the same way.

In the twenty-first century, there have been advances in transportation and technology that make it much easier to produce goods and move them around the world quickly and relatively inexpensively. The development of better information and communications technologies, particularly the internet, has allowed for this inexpensive ease.

In addition to the ease the internet provides, cost-cutting has been another important reason for the growth of globalization. Many well-known companies conduct business in countries around the world. They often open factories in other nations for a variety of economic reasons. Labor may be less expensive in other countries. Less expensive labor saves companies money. International trade can also makes it more appealing to manufacture goods in the countries that consume them. This cuts down on shipping costs.

As mentioned before, Apple products are only designed in California. They are actually largely manufactured in Shenzhen, China. The cost of the skilled labor required to make an iPhone, for instance, is much cheaper in China than it is in the United States. For that reason, Apple has

In 2017, Apple released the iPhone X. The phone, like most Apple products, was mostly assembled in China.

Chinese laborers make these phones. This money-saving practice is called outsourcing. In fact, outsourcing also saves the consumer money. Since the product is cheaper to make, the company can sell it for a reduced price and still make a profit. Some estimate that if the iPhone X were made in the United States, it would have to be sold for $2,000, nearly double the cost.

Is It a Good or Bad Thing?

Globalization is a complex issue. There are many people who are supportive of globalization. They believe it is a way to help poorer countries develop their economies and improve the lives of their citizens. But there are also those who are against globalization. They think it ultimately hurts the workers and economies of both the home country and its foreign trading partners. It's possible that both sides are right.

The Pros

Those who support globalization have a number of reasons they think it helps the world. They believe that it has led to an increase in communication between people. They also believe it has had a positive impact on our environment, as international organizations work together to combat some of our global environmental issues. Others see the movement of people who choose to live and work in other countries as a positive effect as well.

Supporters of globalization believe that it can increase economic success and offer opportunities for countries with weaker economies. These opportunities can include an increase in the jobs available and higher pay for workers. Globalization can also lead to enhanced freedoms for the people living in countries with economic hardships. For example, workers might organize a union that will represent them in order to gain pay increases and better benefits, such as health care.

Advocates also say that globalization can lead to the more efficient distribution of resources. For instance,

In Kenya, shipping containers are used to create solar-powered internet cafes. These provide internet access to people living in rural areas.

the spread of technology has been a positive outcome of globalization. Companies are establishing factories and offices in different countries, bringing with them new technologies that might not reach some underdeveloped countries otherwise.

More important, globalization has helped to improve living conditions in less developed countries. Many people

THE SILK ROAD

Although we often think of globalization in the modern era, it has its roots in ancient trade relations, like the Silk Road. The Silk Road was a network of trade routes that spanned Eurasia and some northeast African countries. The network took its name from one of the most transported goods: silk. The fabric was first produced in China. Soon, other countries were eager to get their hands on it. Since the second century BCE, China has exported silk.

Along the Silk Road, however, other goods, beliefs, and services were also exchanged. This led to economic and cultural globalization. For instance, the route many traders traveled passed through India. Chinese people became familiar with Buddhism, a religion that originated in India, through Silk Road exchanges.

Although the economic and cultural effects of the Silk Road were sizeable, they weren't the only types of globalization that were at play. As Rome lost the territories it controlled in Asia, there was political globalization. New groups rose to power, which made the Silk Road unsafe for some traders. Countries had to work together to ensure necessary trade still occurred.

Buddhism is based on the teachings of Siddhartha Gautama, or the Buddha. In 2018, there were over 488 million Buddhists worldwide.

who didn't have access to basic necessities now have better food choices, basic shelter, and decent clothing. In the twenty-first century, some of the world's fastest economic development has occurred in historically poorer countries such as India, China, and Indonesia. This is because large companies have moved production or customer service centers to these countries. These moves open thousands of jobs. As people find more and better employment, they are better able to spend money on goods and services, which strengthens an economy.

Additionally, globalization encourages the movement of people. The migration of people is not new. For centuries, people have left their homes in search of better opportunities, both in and outside of their own countries. Globalization has just added a new dimension. As businesses expand to include operations in foreign countries, migration becomes an option for many. For instance, someone working for Google in New York City could perhaps relocate to the company's offices in London, Buenos Aires, Moscow, or Bangkok.

The Cons

The term "anti-globalization" is used to describe the opinions of people and groups that oppose this type of global expansion. Some countries may adopt anti-globalization stances, making it harder for people, goods, and culture to spread to and from those countries. Those who are anti-globalization believe it can have a negative impact on employment, culture, and the environment.

People who are concerned with the negative effects of globalization often point to labor conditions as a clear issue. Globalization has given companies the opportunity to establish themselves in other nations. Some companies have used this as a way to save money and pay workers less than they deserve. This unfortunate practice is magnified by the fact that some countries do not have strong health, labor, and safety laws in place. These types of laws can protect workers from workplace hazards or limit the number of hours a company can require them to work. Without these protections, companies are able to abuse their employees. While these workers are free to leave their jobs, they may not have another job to go to.

Similarly, opponents of globalization point to how these global companies contribute to the world's poverty. The large amount of cheap labor in poorer nations gives wealthier ones no reason to solve the problem of economic inequality between nations.

In the same way that health, labor, and safety laws can differ from country to country, so, too, can environmental regulations. While globalization can help inspire the solving of our environmental problems, it can also add to them. For example, some countries allow businesses

Drawbacks to globalization can include companies mistreating employees by paying them low wages, making them work long hours, or forcing them to work in poor conditions.

to be less concerned with pollution. They do not limit the amount of pollution that companies can generate. This can cause widespread environmental dangers.

There are also negative effects that are less concrete and, some would consider, less clearly dangerous. For instance, opponents of globalization worry about its effect on cultural identities. A loss of cultural identity can occur when two or more cultures collide. There is a risk that each country could lose some of the aspects of its heritage that make it unique. Although it may seem like a small thing, cultural heritage is how our ancestors learned to work the land and grow food. Without these diverse identities, we'd lose some of what makes our world so fascinating.

The Reality

The positives of globalization often seem to outweigh the negatives. It can increase the wealth of poorer countries. It creates employment. It can result in global problem-solving through shared approaches to pressing issues like protecting the environment or curing deadly diseases. It brings nations together to help one another in times of crisis. Globalization has the potential to make our world a better, more cooperative, and more peaceful place.

The reality is, though, that it's easy to see the positives because globalization affects so many parts of our lives. It can lead to an increase in the variety of products we buy, the kinds of foods we eat, the languages we speak, the kinds of cars we drive, and the places we travel to. It would be hard for us to imagine our lives without globalization at this point. For that reason, it remains important to have a balanced view of its effects.

CHAPTER 3

A CLOSER LOOK

Think about all the items you own, from your clothes and toys to your books, movies, and video games. Many of these products were created, designed, manufactured, or developed in foreign countries. Globalization has opened up a worldwide market for companies; however, as we've seen, it affects far more than what we can purchase. It allows people worldwide to work together to solve a range of problems, from diseases to environmental issues. Again, despite the positive effects of many of these advancements that have been made possible through globalization, it is important to also consider the drawbacks. Let's take a closer look at both.

Opposite: Often, clothes sold in the United States are made in other countries like Indonesia, China, Vietnam, and Bangladesh.

The Environmental Impact

Globalization has drawn attention to the state of the environment, which affects all of us. Environmental concerns include melting glaciers and ice caps, increased air pollution, dwindling supplies of freshwater, and the changing climate. For example, the West Coast of the United States is affected by the air pollution that is created in China and other Asian countries. Tiny airborne particles of pollution drift over the Pacific Ocean from coal-fired power plants, dust storms, and diesel trucks in Asia. This is harmful to the air and water quality in American cities like San Francisco. This environmental issue is, in part, a result of cultural and economic globalization. In other words, the companies moving jobs to China are responsible for some of the increased air pollution. These companies are moving to China for cheaper labor so that they can save money while churning out products that are in demand all over the world.

China isn't the only culprit when it comes to high levels of pollution and energy consumption. Globalization has led to an increase in energy use worldwide. With these advances in technology, people use more energy to power tools, machines, cars, appliances, and manufacturing plants.

There are many different types of energy. There are fossil fuels, which are formed in the earth from plant or animal remains. Oil is one of the most popular examples of fossil fuels. Renewable energy, also known as alternative energy, is another type. It uses existing energy, as well as natural processes, to generate more for future use. For instance, solar power, hydropower, and wind power are all examples of renewable energy.

Although there are many renewable energy sources, they are often costly to set up. For that reason, much of the world still relies heavily on fossil fuels. The use of them, however, puts an enormous and growing strain on Earth's resources and health. The burning of fossil fuels leads to the release of carbon dioxide and other gases into the atmosphere, which surrounds and protects the planet. These gases trap heat from Earth's surface in our atmosphere. In fact, these gases, called greenhouse gases, radiate the heat back to Earth's surface. This increased heat leads to global warming, or the increased average temperature of Earth's surface. This change to the climate causes melting ice caps and rising sea levels, threatening our livelihood.

Something positive that has come out of the dangerous effects globalization and manufacturing have had on the environment is that there have been several worldwide organizations that are trying to develop international environmental policies. These are examples of political globalization.

The Effect of Increased Communication

Thanks to globalization, there has been an increase in information flowing between countries. People around the world are more connected to each other than ever before. Both the internet and satellite television have made it possible to read newspapers, watch news broadcasts, and see movies and shows originating in foreign countries. As societies and economies embrace new communication technologies, the peoples of the world become a closer-knit community.

Let's look back at a historical event that shows how news can impact the world and connect us all. The day is September 11, 2001. You and your family live in New York City. Today, however, you are all in Paris, France, on a trip. It is early afternoon in Europe. Your family decides to take a break from museums and goes back to the hotel room. You turn on the television and flip through the channels. Suddenly, on one of the news stations, you see an image of the Twin Towers of the World Trade Center in New York City on fire. You sit and watch history unfold. You and your family might be alone in your hotel room in Paris, but at the same time you are connected to millions of others who are watching the very same images all around the world. You are all sharing the same experience at the same time.

On September 11, 2001, people worldwide watched the events related to the terrorist attacks in the United States unfold. Now, this memorial exists to commemorate the lives lost in New York City.

Now, imagine what it must have been like on December 7, 1941. On this day, during World War II, Japanese forces attacked Pearl Harbor in Hawaii. Television was in its infancy in the early 1940s. Commercial stations like ABC were just beginning to get broadcasting licenses from the government. It took hours for news of the surprise attack to reach most Americans, mostly through their radios. It took days or even weeks before the full story, with photographs of burning and sinking battleships, made it into newspaper articles worldwide.

Globalization has made it possible for magazines, newspapers, and other news outlets to share information about global events quickly. CNN, founded in 1980, has international divisions that deliver the news in Spanish, Turkish, Korean, and Japanese. Major news publications, such as *Time* magazine, have international broadcast networks. Both global reporting and international offices increase our understanding of those who live in different parts of the world.

Although information is literally at our fingertips these days, some experts have expressed concern about our access to news twenty-four hours a day. Similarly, some worry that seeing images of 9/11 or victims of the Syrian Civil War on television actually desensitizes viewers. In other words, viewers are so used to seeing violence and disturbing content that they are numb to it.

In the mid-twentieth century, it took days or weeks for photos of the attack on Pearl Harbor to make it into newspapers around the world.

QUICK Q&A

Is globalization a new concept?

Not really. Globalization may be moving at a much faster pace today, but it has been around for thousands of years. Throughout history, nations have exchanged goods with other countries and established companies on foreign soil. This international exchange of goods and services is known as trade, and it is a major component of globalization.

So why does globalization feel like something that started in the twentieth century?

It sort of did. Although the components of globalization are not necessarily new, the term itself is. Theodore Levitt, a Harvard Business School professor, is credited with coining the term. He first used it in a 1983 *Harvard Business Review* article entitled "The Globalization of

Markets." A *New York Times* article printed after his death in 2006 explains that Levitt understood globalization as "the changes in technology and social behaviors that allow multinational companies like Coca-Cola and McDonald's to sell the same products worldwide."

Since globalization has such a far reach, could it lead to world peace?

Probably not. Globalization leads to the spread of cultures, languages, ideas, and businesses. But it does not mean that people around the world are always ready and willing to welcome foreign influences. The mere exchange of money, goods, and services does not necessarily eliminate long-standing suspicions or grudges between nations. Sometimes, globalization can actually increase hard feelings or resentment when people feel their native culture is under attack by a foreign one or their jobs are being sent to other countries.

If they are numb to it, then it is possible they will do less to change things like poor conditions for workers in other countries.

The Cultural Impact

Globalization can expose people to new ideas and experiences. As these new ideas or beliefs are adopted, the values and traditions of a culture can change and evolve. As a result, if the change is extreme or sudden enough, it may result in a loss of cultural identity.

Food is an area in which this occurs most commonly. In many countries, food is an integral part of culture's identity. But with globalization, outside influences can change the role that food plays. Take, for example, the American coffee company Starbucks. Originally, Starbucks was a company that just sold coffee beans. It did not sell brewed coffee in its stores. This all changed when the head of the company, Howard Schultz, traveled to Italy. While there, he observed the importance of coffee to the Italians.

Coffee in Italy is more than a drink. It is part of the Italian way of life. Italians sit in cafés and truly enjoy a cup of coffee. In the United States, however, it is common for people to buy a cup and take it with them to the office or to drink it in the car while driving to work. Schultz saw an opportunity to change the way that Americans drink

Coffee shop culture was brought to the United States from Italy, where drinking coffee is often a social occasion.

coffee. He made Starbucks cafés places to sit, relax, and sample different brews of coffee while casually meeting with friends.

The cultural diversity offered by globalization can be wonderful. For example, millions of Americans can now sit and enjoy coffee over light conversation at a local Starbucks and other coffee shops modeled in a communal way. However, it can also have its drawbacks. In 2018, Starbucks opened its first café in Milan, Italy. Could Italians now start to embrace the grab-and-go model so familiar to Americans? Would they lose the cultural staple of people enjoying a coffee *insieme*—Italian for "together"?

The Effect on Public Health

Globalization promotes both the rapid spread and the effective treatment of highly contagious diseases. Advanced transportation technology now means that people travel farther. This greater movement of goods and people increases the chance for the spread of diseases around the world. Just like products, diseases like influenza, malaria, and tuberculosis can travel across oceans and national borders to infect more people. For example, mosquitoes that carry malaria have been found on planes thousands of miles from their primary habitats.

While globalization is responsible for the spread of some of these diseases, it can provide the solution as well. It can improve access to medicines, medical information, and training that can help treat or cure diseases. Drug companies and governments now have the ability to ship medicine to remote parts of the world affected by epidemics, or widespread occurrences of infectious diseases. This means that these companies are able to provide medical care to areas that they might not have been able to reach before.

A Balancing Act

As you can see, globalization is a delicate balance. Although it has done the world a lot of good, there are also reasons countries try to regulate its effects and reach.

CHAPTER 4

THE GLOBAL MELTING POT

One of the best things about globalization is that it allows people to experience different cultures. Just because someone was born in France does not mean that she is limited to speaking French, eating French food, reading French books, and watching French films. A French person—or an American, or an Italian, or a Chinese person—can eat apple pie, pizza, and lo mein all in the same day. She can listen to bhangra, a type of South Asian music that incorporates elements of disco and hip-hop, or country. She can play baseball or practice yoga, an Indian meditation practice. She can read books and magazines in any number of languages. Exploring

Opposite: Yoga is a meditative practice that originated in India. It is now practiced all over the world.

and experiencing other cultures makes our lives richer and more exciting.

Americanization

As American companies expand into foreign countries, the idea of Americanization has emerged as a concern. Americanization is a term that describes the dominating and transformative influence the United States has on other cultures. For example, American television, film, and music are considered to be the biggest agents of Americanization in other countries. According to a 2015 study of eighteen countries, *NCIS* is one of the most popular television shows worldwide. An American soap opera, *The Bold and the Beautiful*, is popular among Italians, while South Koreans preferred the drama of *Scandal*.

The Walt Disney Company is an example of American culture's reach throughout the world. The company is a massive global corporation. It is one of the largest media, entertainment, and merchandising enterprises in the world. Brothers Walt and Roy Disney founded it in 1923. Originally, it was an animation studio, where cartoon movies like *Cinderella*, *Snow White*, and *Fantasia* were drawn. It has now become one of the biggest Hollywood studios and has a fleet of cruise ships in addition to selling clothes, toys, and other consumer products. It is also the owner of twelve theme parks around the world.

When Americanization Meets Globalization

Based on the success of the Disney World and Disneyland amusement parks in the United States, the Walt Disney Company decided to explore the idea of building theme parks in other countries. It first established a theme park in Tokyo in 1983. Based on its success, the company built other parks, like Disneyland Paris in 1992 and Hong Kong Disneyland in 2005.

When the company first decided to build these theme parks, much consideration was given to each country's

Disneyland Paris, originally called Euro Disney, opened in 1992. In its first twenty-five years, the park welcomed over 250 million visitors.

culture. The company wanted to figure out how to best respect each country's culture while introducing the population to the very American Disney phenomenon. For example, Disney representatives sampled lots of local foods to decide what to offer at the theme parks' restaurants and concession stands. They tried to learn the local and national culture in order to make sure that the theme parks accurately reflected each country in a respectful and sensitive way.

When Disney was building the park in Paris, the company hired a panel of European consultants, or cultural experts. These consultants included individuals from France, Switzerland, England, and Germany. Disney learned from this group that Europeans do not like to stand in line for their food. So, the company needed to adjust the way that it designed and operated the food courts and restaurants at its Paris location. It also decided to have more restaurants and fewer snack food options because Europeans do not snack as much as Americans do. Europeans also linger over meals longer than most American diners and prefer to eat outside when the weather is nice. So, when Disney was designing eating areas, it planned for more than 2,100 outdoor seats.

When designing Hong Kong Disneyland, the company took similar cultural differences into consideration. They paid special attention to things that would make its Chinese

The Hong Kong Disneyland grand opening in 2005 featured culturally relevant entertainment such as Chinese lion dancers.

visitors feel welcome. For example, designers were careful to include the principles of feng shui, which is the Chinese art of placing objects in harmony with their environment.

In addition to being conscious of the cultural aspects, Disney also tries to ensure these theme parks are welcoming to international guests. These parks employ people that speak several languages, and they feature signs and maps in many different languages as well. In this way, the company fully embraces globalization in its parks.

The Melting Pot

Although we've talked a lot about how the United States influences other countries, other countries influence the

POLITICAL GLOBALIZATION AND TSUNAMI RELIEF

Remember, although economic and cultural globalization are what most people consider when thinking of globalization, political globalization has a huge effect on people's lives as well.

On December 26, 2004, an earthquake in the Indian Ocean caused a tsunami, a series of massive waves that

In 2004, a devastating tsunami hit parts of southern Asia. The international community rallied around the affected countries to help.

can cause immense flooding and destruction. Particularly hard-hit were India, Indonesia, Sri Lanka, and Thailand. More than 225,000 people were killed, tens of thousands were injured or went missing, and a least a million found themselves homeless. The world's response to this tragedy is an example of political globalization.

Governments and companies from around the world provided help to the countries affected by the natural disaster. More than fifty-five countries offered military help and financial aid. In addition, millions of people donated money to help, and companies worldwide offered their support. Drug companies like Pfizer and Bristol-Myers Squibb provided medical supplies and medications. Beverage companies such as Iceland Spring Water supplied drinking water. And humanitarian organizations like the International Red Cross and the United Nations donated supplies and services, sent volunteers, or raised money to help the tsunami victims rebuild their homes and communities.

culture of the United States just as much. This is not a new phenomenon. The United States has long absorbed influences from around the world. It has roots and ties to the cultures of its former colonial masters: France, Spain, the Netherlands, and Great Britain. The United States' long history of immigration has expanded the range of influences dramatically. Immigration is when people move to a new country in hopes of making it their new permanent home.

The United States is a nation founded by immigrants. In fact, it is defined by the immigrant experience. The United States is often referred to as a melting pot where many cultures are mixed together to form a new identity. As such, the country provides a great example of how cultures come into contact, trade influences, and ultimately create something original and powerful. Such is the case with the all-American blue jean.

Levi Strauss is the creator of blue jeans. He was a German immigrant who came to the United States and settled in San Francisco. He created jeans by combining denim cloth, which was originally woven in a French town, with a style of pants worn by sailors from Genoa, Italy. This style of Italian trousers was called genes. This means that Levi's jeans are, in fact, an American twist on French fabric and Italian style by a German designer. What could be a better example of globalization? This is just one of many instances that demonstrate how distinct cultures spread, mix, and become popular in different parts of the world.

Sports often spread across the globe and become fixtures in their new homelands. Many of the world's most popular sports, most notably soccer, came by way of Britain or Latin America. Both football and baseball have at least some of their origins in England. Asian martial arts like judo, karate, and kickboxing are now widely practiced by people of all ages worldwide. Yoga, which originated in India, has also swept the world.

Globalization and Migration

Although we often talk about globalization in terms of countries' cultural identities, products, and international organizations, people are actually a huge part of globalization. In the twenty-first century, people are increasingly nomadic, meaning they are comfortable moving from place to place or even from country to country.

Many are leaving their homes, excitedly seeking new opportunities in new countries. However, others leave home out of necessity. They can find no work where they live. If they hope to support their families and survive, they must seek employment in other countries. According to the World Bank, in December 2015, there were over 250 million international migrants.

ANNUAL MEETINGS
2018 | indonesia
INTERNATIONAL MONETARY FUND
WORLD BANK GROUP

CHAPTER 5

PEOPLE AT THE HEART OF GLOBALIZATION

Just as businesses have become globalized, so, too, have workers. The migration of people across borders is not new. People have always left their homes in search of better opportunities, both within and outside of their own countries. Globalization has added a new dimension to this movement of workers, however. As businesses expand to include operations in foreign countries, globalization has made migration a necessity for many people. Their jobs at home may get sent overseas, where people may be willing to work for less money. This leaves the people who used to work for the company unemployed. There may be no jobs in their area anymore, so they are forced

Opposite: The International Monetary Fund is an international organization that brings world leaders together to discuss global economic concerns such as poverty and economic development.

to travel to where the jobs are. This may mean moving to another town, county, state, or even country.

Responses to Increased US Immigration

More and more people are immigrating to the United States. Since 1990, the number of foreign-born US residents has risen. In 2017, almost 14 percent of the US population was made up of people born in another country. Many of these people are coming from Mexico, China, and India.

This increase of immigration to the United States has sparked outrage and fear among some Americans. Some people fear losing their jobs to an immigrant willing to work for less money. Others are not comfortable with the customs or culture of newly arrived residents.

Some people who feel this way believe that borders should be closed to all new immigration. Other believe that only people from certain countries should be allowed into the United States. For example, during the 2016 presidential campaign, Donald Trump ran on the promise he would build a wall between Mexico and the United States. This wall would be built to limit Mexican immigration into the United States. Similarly, once he was president, Trump took steps to limit immigration from several predominately Muslim countries.

What gets lost sometimes on that side of the immigration debate is the fact that all Americans who are not Native Americans are the descendants of immigrants. The ancestors of most Americans entered the stream of globalization. Most of them chose to leave their homes for better economic, political, or personal opportunities in a new land. These early agents of globalization brought their cultural traditions with them. They contributed to a new American culture that preached freedom, liberty, industry, and tolerance. Today's immigrants are adding new layers of richness to this culture.

Global Responses to Increased Immigration

The United States is not the only country that deals with waves of immigration due to globalization. In 2015 and 2016, migrants flocked to European countries. These individuals left behind unstable governments and political unrest in their home countries. In the years that European countries dealt with what they called a migrant crisis, people were fleeing countries like Syria, which was in the midst of a devastating civil war. The war displaced over ten million people. Four million of those people left Syria in hopes of finding more stable homes and jobs elsewhere. Although globalization meant that people could more easily move between countries, some

European nations found it hard to sustain the growing populations of immigrants. Similarly, these migrants often had difficulty finding work.

The Realities of Immigration

It may sound like it would be exciting for people to relocate to a new country in search of work or a relief for them to leave behind political uncertainty. However,

In 2016, refugees set up camp at Greece's Port of Piraeus, the country's largest seaport, in hopes of entering the country.

the reality is that many people put their lives at risk to move to these new countries. Many are from families that cannot afford to collectively pack up and fly to a new location. They must travel by other, more dangerous means. For instance, several hundred people each year die trying to enter the United States through the Mexican border. Similarly, people flooded the Mediterranean Sea during the European migrant crisis in hopes of sailing to a new life. Too many never made it to the distant shores of prosperity, or good fortune. It is estimated that over twelve thousand individuals died trying to cross the Mediterranean between 2013 and 2017.

The Realities of the Global Workplace

Once people survive these journeys to new countries, however, their hopes and dreams aren't always fulfilled. Sometimes there aren't jobs available, or the ones that are available pay terribly low wages. Take the Apple company, for instance. If skilled laborers from the United States moved to work in the Foxconn factory responsible for some iPhone manufacturing in China, they would be making less money than they would in the United States.

Even people who are from the places where international companies have set up factories find this new life of globalization difficult. For example, some

A FEW MORE FACTS

- Brand-name goods sold in the United States—whether they are toys, clothing, or electronics—are often made in foreign countries. The reason for this is that labor is often cheaper in foreign countries. When an American company pays less to make goods, it means that they can charge less for them. It also means that the company makes more money for its goods because it is paying its workers less. There are companies, however, that pride themselves on creating products that are locally made. This often means that the workers are being paid fair wages. Additionally, this can also mean that the materials are sourced and made into products in environmentally friendly ways.

- Another thing to remember is that globalization is not equally distributed. Although it can lead to jobs in new countries, there are only certain countries in which companies set up factories. These companies are usually setting up factories in nations with existing industrial economies. So, for instance, international car manufacturing companies like BMW and Toyota have factories in countries like Germany, the United States, and Thailand. It is unlikely that these corporations will open factories in Nepal or the Central African Republic, two of the world's poorest countries, even if these nations would benefit from the influx of jobs.

Chinese workers refer to Foxconn as a trap. Employees live on a large, secure, city-like campus where they eat, sleep, and work. Foxconn boasts free housing for their workers but then charges them high prices for utilities like electricity and water. Some employees report long hours, public shaming for poor work, low pay, and withheld wages. Some say they suffer from depression because of these conditions. In spite of the increased jobs offered by globalization, the reality is that it is still hard for many people around the world to just get by.

The Future of Our Globalized World

We will have to continue to consider the effects of globalization on people as we move forward into the future. For all of its wonders, unchecked globalization can lead to immigration crises, as people flock to countries where they can find work. Many experts believe that the current rate of globalization is not sustainable. As we expand global economies and production to meet demand, we are straining our environmental resources. The more strain we put on our resources, the greater we affect climate change. In order to continue to have a livable planet, it will be important to keep working to combat the environmental effects of our increasingly industrialized world.

In addition to protecting the planet on which we live, we must also protect our fellow global citizens. Although globalization has done a lot to lift people out of poverty

The bulk of people moving to Europe during the wave of immigration in 2015 were fleeing political unrest and searching for economic opportunities.

and provide the world with a range of technologies, we must ensure that the workers responsible for the marvels of globalization are treated humanely.

GLOSSARY

Americanization A term that describes the dominating and transformative influence the United States has on the cultures of other countries.

capital Another word for money or wealth, especially when used for investments and to build businesses.

climate change The shifts in Earth's weather patterns.

cultural globalization The deepening of international social connectedness through the exchange of cultural ideas and products, such as movies and music.

division of labor The breakdown or separating out of jobs in a manufacturing process to increase efficiency.

economic globalization The exchange of goods, services, and money across international markets, establishing a global community.

export To send products made in one country to another country.

globalization The increased international influence or movement of people, knowledge, ideas, products, and money.

global warming The increased average temperature of Earth's surface.

greenhouse gases Gases like carbon dioxide that trap heat in Earth's atmosphere and radiate it back to Earth's surface; these types of gases contribute to global warming.

immigration The act of moving to another country with the intention of making it a permanent residence.

import To bring foreign products into a country.

melting pot A term, popularized by British writer Israel Zangwill in 1908, for the mixing of a variety of cultures into one identity, typically through immigration.

migration The movement of people from one country, place, or locality to another.

nomadic Wandering from place to place, usually without a specific destination.

outsource To hire foreign workers for a job instead of hiring workers within the company's home country.

political globalization A system of international governments and multinational organizations that work together for the common global good.

renewable energy Electricity that comes from a source that can be replenished and is typically environmentally friendly, like the sun, wind, and water.

tariff A government tax on imports or exports.

transmission The spread of something, such as ideas or diseases.

FURTHER INFORMATION

Books

Idzikowski, Lisa. *Globalization and Free Trade*. Introducing Issues with Opposing Viewpoints. New York: Greenhaven Press, 2018.

Mann, Charles C., and Rebecca Stefoff. *1493 for Young People: From Columbus's Voyage to Globalization*. New York: Triangle Square, 2016.

Mooney, Carla. *Globalization: Why We Care About Faraway Events*. Inquire & Investigate. White River Junction, VT: Nomad Press, 2018.

Perritano, John. *Trade, Economic Life, and Globalization*. The Making of the Modern World: 1945 to the Present. Broomall, PA: Mason Crest, 2016.

Websites

Globalization101

http://www.globalization101.org

This website provides a breakdown and overview of the concepts related to globalization.

International Education and Resource Network USA

http://us.iearn.org

This website helps students "connect and learn with their international peers" to inspire "global collaboration and transformative learning."

Videos

Globalization and Trade and Poverty: Crash Course Economics #16

https://www.youtube.com/watch?v=9MpVjxxpExM

This video gives a brief explanation of how globalization affects trade and poverty in addition to explaining the pros and cons of globalized economies.

TEDxAix: The Myth of Globalisation

https://www.youtube.com/watch?v=xUYNB4a8d2U

Peter Alfandary, a lawyer, discusses the importance of understanding cultural differences in our globalized world.

Organizations

Centre for Research on Globalization
PO Box 55019
11 Notre-Dame Ouest
Montreal, QC H2Y 4A7
Canada
Website: http://www.globalresearch.ca

The Centre for Research on Globalization is a group of writers, scholars, journalists, and activists. The organization "publishes news articles, commentary, background research and analysis on a broad range of issues, focusing on social, political, economic, cultural, strategic and environmental issues."

International Development Research Centre

PO Box 8500
Ottawa, ON K1G 3H9
Canada
(613) 236-6163
Website: http://www.idrc.ca

This multinational organization helps developing countries use science and technology to find practical, long-term solutions to the social, economic, and environmental problems they face.

International Forum on Globalization

1009 General Kennedy Avenue, #2
San Francisco, CA 94129
(415) 561-7650
Website: http://www.ifg.org

This research and educational institution is composed of leading activists, economists, scholars, and researchers who provide analyses and critiques on the cultural, social, political, and environmental impacts of economic globalization.

Niehaus Center for Globalization and Governance

Woodrow Wilson School, Princeton University
Robertson Hall
Princeton, NJ 08544-1013
(609) 258-0181
Website: https://niehaus.princeton.edu

Founded in 2004, the center is committed to encouraging "ties between the academic and policy communities involved in globalization and international governance issues" in order to tackle contemporary issues and prepare future policy makers for the types of decisions they will face.

United Nations

405 E 42nd Street (46th Street & 1st Avenue)
New York, NY 10017
(212) 963-4475
Website: http://www.un.org/en/index.html

Established in 1945, this international organization was developed to support the global community in many different ways.

World Trade Organization

Centre William Rappard
Rue de Lausanne 154
CH-1211 Geneva 21
Switzerland
Email: enquires@wto.org
Website: http://www.wto.org

The World Trade Organization is the only international organization that deals with the rules of trade between nations.

SELECTED BIBLIOGRAPHY

Adalian, Josef. "The Most Popular US TV Shows in 18 Countries Around the World." *Vulture*, December 2, 2015. http://www.vulture.com/2015/12/most-popular-us-tv-shows-around-the-world.html.

Bajekal, Naina. "The 5 Big Questions About Europe's Migrant Crisis." *Time*, September 9, 2015. http://time.com/4026380/europe-migrant-crisis-questions-refugees.

Bhagwati, Jagdish. *In Defense of Globalization*. New York: Oxford University Press, 2007.

Chappell, Bill. "Smog In Western US Starts Out as Pollution in Asia, Researchers Say." NPR, March 3, 2017. https://www.npr.org/sections/thetwo-way/2017/03/03/518323094/rise-in-smog-in-western-u-s-is-blamed-on-asias-air-pollution.

Cook, Jesselyn. "More Than 3,000 Migrants Have Died Crossing the Mediterranean This Year." *Huffington Post*, November 28, 2017. https://www.huffingtonpost.com/entry/mediterranean-3000-migrants-dead_us_5a1d7d88e4b0e2ddcbb2d99c.

Eitzen, D. Stanley, and Maxine Baca Zinn. *Globalization: The Transformation of Social Worlds*. Boston: Wadsworth, 2008.

Feder, Barnaby. "Theodore Levitt, 81, Who Coined the Term 'Globalization,' Is Dead." *New York Times*,

July 6, 2006. https://www.nytimes.com/2006/07/06/business/06levitt.html?module=ArrowsNav&contentCollection=Business%20Day&action=keypress&region=FixedLeft&pgtype=article.

Friedman, Thomas L. *The Lexus and the Olive Tree: Understanding Globalization.* Norwell, MA: Anchor Press, 2000.

Ghosh, Mousumi. "Silk Road: A Glance at Archaic Globalization." Silk Routes: Heritage, Trade, Practice. Accessed September 30, 2018. https://iwp.uiowa.edu/silkroutes/city/kolkata/text/silk-road-glance-archaic-globalization.

Graham, Jefferson. "Why Not Build an iPhone in the USA?" *USA Today*, January 20, 2018. https://www.usatoday.com/story/tech/talkingtech/2018/01/20/why-not-build-iphone-usa/1047294001/.

Lubin, Gus. "13 Disturbing Facts About McDonald's." *Fiscal Times*, April 30, 2012. http://www.thefiscaltimes.com/Articles/2012/04/30/13-Disturbing-Facts-About-McDonalds.

Marling, William H. *How American Is Globalization?* Baltimore: Johns Hopkins University Press, 2006.

Merchant, Brian. *The One Device: The Secret History of the iPhone.* New York: Little, Brown and Company, 2017.

"Migrant Deaths Along US-Mexico Border Remain High Despite Drop in Crossings." UN News,

February 6, 2018. https://news.un.org/en/story/2018/02/1002101.

Sorensen, Jeff. "24-Hour News Killed Journalism." *Huffington Post*, August 20, 2012. https://www.huffingtonpost.com/jeff-sorensen/24-hour-news_b_1813081.html. Stiglitz, Joseph E. *Globalization and Its Discontents*. New York: W. W. Norton & Co., 2003.

"What Is the Paris Agreement?" United Nations Framework Convention on Climate Change. Accessed September 22, 2018. https://unfccc.int/process-and-meetings/the-paris-agreement/what-is-the-paris-agreement.

INDEX

Page numbers in **boldface** refer to images.

ABOUT THE AUTHOR

Chet'la Sebree is a writer, editor, and researcher. She has written and edited several books for Cavendish Square Publishing, including one on the Great Depression. She has degrees in English and creative writing from the University of Richmond and American University, respectively. She is from the Mid-Atlantic region.